Early Morning Meditations

Early Morning Meditations

Rev. Peter L. Chabot, M.M.

gatekeeper press
Columbus, Ohio

Early Morning Meditations

Published by Gatekeeper Press
2167 Stringtown Rd, Suite 109
Columbus, OH 43123-2989
www.GatekeeperPress.com

Copyright © 2021 by Rev. Peter L. Chabot, M.M.
All rights reserved. Neither this book, nor any parts within it may be sold or reproduced in any form or by any electronic or mechanical means, including information storage and retrieval systems without permission in writing from the author. The only exception is by a reviewer, who may quote short excerpts in a review.

ISBN (paperback): 9781662908842

He could have been
a professional artist,
he was that good,
and gone to work for
The Saturday Evening Post.

He could have been
a professional baseball player,
he was that good,
and gone to work for the
Boston Red Sox.

He could have been
a professional magician,
he was that good,
and gone to work in
Las Vegas.

He could have been
a professional flim-flam man,
he was that good,
and gone to work selling
pyramid schemes.

Instead he became a priest,
and went to work for God.
He was that good.

—Dan Chabot

Madonna of the Rosary
Michelangelo Merisi da
Caravaggio
1571-1610

people living
in isolated
communities
along the
Amazon
headwaters
receive messages
by transistor
radio

telegraphic
announcements
are broadcast
to dozens
of these places
every evening
for an hour

they range
from news items
to matters of
life and death

batteries
are costly
and so
their energy
is conserved
as much as
possible
for the
messages

during the day
you can see
them placed

in sunlight
on windowsills
soaking up
a precious dose
of solar energy

there is a
lesson here
concerning
our own
limited energies

to conserve them
for the
really important
messages
from God
in our
daily lives

help us
o Lord
to hear
and heed
your Word
and to avoid
the harmful
influences
that keep us
from You

Rev. Peter L. Chabot, M.M.

Traubenmadonna
Lucas Cranach the Elder
1472-1553

along the edges
of sandy beaches
desert borders
barren places

the sand reed
grows in
great profusion

there is a
certain beauty
to them
especially
when a
rippling breeze
passes through

their roots
go deep
holding erosion
at bay

they provide
shelter and
protection
for smaller plants

often overlooked
their usefulness
even necessity
is taken
for granted

yet without them
desert sands
would replace

vegetation
and turn
fertile fields
into barrenness
and desolation

a daily schedule
of prayer
plays a
similar role
in the spiritual life

much like the way
nourishment
and exercise
are needed
for one's health

what oxygen
is to the diver
practice
to the musician
study
to the scholar

so too
building
into one's life
a solid
regular
prayer life
is paramount
not just
for growth
but for survival

Madonna and Child
Giotto Di Bondone
1266-1337

I
in his book
Man's Search
For Meaning
Victor Frankl
chronicles
his harrowing
experiences
in a
concentration
camp

to have someone
or something
to live for
is significant
to whether
you survive
or not

thus evolved
logotherapy
having an
outside source
towards which
one's energies
are directed

wherein
one is freed
from the confines
of self
and finds
meaning outside

in Christ
we find meaning
freedom
from bondage
to sin
ignorance
addiction
despair
even death

in the
new life
in Him
the Holy Spirit
comes into
our lives

we become
temples of God
as the Holy Spirit
dwells within
and
all is changed
all is made new

come
Holy Spirit

Rev. Peter L. Chabot, M.M.

Madonna and Child
Bartolomeo Vivanni
1432-1499

the effect
of a pinch
of salt
is out of all
proportion
to what it
looks like

when you
sprinkle salt
on something
it becomes
invisible
does not
call attention
to itself

long journeys
are made possible
when meat
and fish are
heavily salted
as it preserves
them
from corruption

immerse
a bent and
twisted wire
into a salt lake
and in a
half hour
there will appear
a figurine
of sparkling beauty

salt purifies
seasons
adds flavor

in blessings
salt symbolizes
the grace of Christ
and heavenly wisdom

have salt
in yourselves
and be
at peace
with
one another

Lord Jesus
may the salt
of your grace
save us
from sin
and bestow
the wisdom
and strength
needed
to walk
in your ways

Early Morning Meditations

Madonna and Child
Fra Filippo Lippi
1406-1469

the crowds
had come
and gone
a spacious
meadow
now cobblestoned
to accommodate
the half million
pilgrims who come
to Fatima
every year

going up
into the hills
to the site of
the August apparition
encountering
flocks of sheep
olive trees

a slow
climbing
bus ride
back into
another century
mainly now
like it was
back in 1917

i knelt
before a statue
of Our Lady
and prayed
a decade
of the Rosary
and was immersed
in the aura

of the apparitions
that occurred
here
not all that
long ago

a brief meeting
with Maria
sister of Lucy
listening
to her account
of the miracle
of the sun
her words
tumbling out
like the
sparkling
crystalline waters
of a
mountain stream

reverence
wonder
attend the site
of this
amazing visit
of Heaven's Queen
i go back there
often
in thought
and experience
a deep
spiritual
refreshment

you can too

Rev. Peter L. Chabot, M.M.

Madonna and Child
Guido di Pietro (Fra Angelico)
1387-1455

A captured soldier
smuggled
a book
into prison camp

he slowed
his reading
speed
to a half an hour
per page

to where
he could
feel
the sea breeze
in his face

hear
the sound
of waves

get the feel
of the trade winds

this is a
good way
to do
spiritual
reading

become
a participant
in what
goes on

imagine
the writing

addressed
to you
personally

draw
conclusions
make
resolutions
take
to heart
Scripture
quotes

seek first
the kingdom
of God

what does
it profit
to gain
the whole world
and lose
your soul

help me
o Lord
to make
your presence
more real
in my life

Madonna and Child
Hans Memling
1430-1494

if today
you hear His voice
harden not
your hearts

the folly of
procrastination
is one of the
oldest themes
in literature

remember
the race
between a tortoise
and a hare

the tortoise
passes the
slumbering hare
who
winning easily
decided to
take it easy
slows down
takes a nap
and oversleeps
losing
an opportunity
that may not
come again

the hour is here
the moment
is now
to put into place
a schedule
and habit

of daily prayer
that will sustain
illumine
guide
especially
in those times
when storm clouds
move in
and cause us to
lose our bearings

if today
you hear
His voice
harden not
your hearts

Lord Jesus
you know
how prone
we are
to put things off
firm up
our will
steel our resolve
to keep
in good spiritual shape
so that
when You come again
we may be found
as faithful servants
awaiting
watching for
their Master's return

Rev. Peter L. Chabot, M.M.

Madonna of the Choir
Raphael Santi
1484-1520

T the Old
Testament
is filled
with wars
strife conflict
marching armies
tremendous battles
resounding victories
disastrous defeats
long years
spent in exile

the images
of war and
weaponry also
make their way
into the
New Testament

Paul speaks of
putting on
the armor
of faith
the breastplate
of salvation
as protection
against the
fiery darts
and flying arrows
of the evil one

the great difference
though
in what
many call
the spiritual combat
is that

the battle
has already
been won

we have only
to take up arms
of faith prayer
the sacraments
and enter
the fray
where victory
is assured
as long as we
stay united
to Jesus Christ
the Victor
in this most
important of battles

then the
shouts of victory
so often heard
in days of old
become our own
and the refrain
i will rejoice
in your salvation
o Lord
becomes a
hymn of joy
during our exile
here
and a song
of thanksgiving
through all
eternity

14

The Alba Madonna
Raphael Santi
1484-1520

faith and
prayer
are so
closely linked
together
as to be
inseparable
each depends
upon and is
strengthened
by the other

the poor
in spirit
whose lives
are not filled
with lesser
matters
provide
fertile soil
for faith

prayer then
becomes an
integral part
of their
relationship
with God
not just asking for
something in
times of emergency

but
praying itself
becomes
its own
answer

bringing about
and strengthening
union with God
so that
when requests
are delayed
or answered
in unexpected ways
believing prayer
gratefully accepts
and understands

especially
long delays
for a habit
a custom
a routine
of prayer
is built up
and takes
its place
in the
central structure
of one's life
and becomes
in itself
a gift
in answer
to prayer

Rev. Peter L. Chabot, M.M.

Small Cowper Madonna
Raphael Santi
1484–1520

On our
spiritual journey
we are like
the blind beggar
in the Gospel
praying
Lord
that i may see
when You
asked him
and us
what can I
do for you

Lord that i may see
grant me
the insight
of faith
to know God
to know myself

to live
and experience
your presence
in the new life
faith brings

Lord
that i may see
all peoples
as your children
Lord that i
may see You
in all the
circumstances
of life

and know
that You
are near

may i see You
in trial
and suffering

in grief
and tribulation

may i see You
in times
of need

may You be
my way through
fear and anxiety

may i see You in the
joys
of this life
remembering
that they too
will end

and are but
a glimmer
of those
in the life
to come

Madonna of the Grand Duke
Raphael Santi (Raphael)
1483-1520

Our Father

two words
that tell us
who God is
who we are
and define our
relationship
to each other

who art
in heaven
and also
within
know you
not that
you are
temples
of God

thy kingdom come
interiorly
socially
throughout eternity

thy will
be done
in His will
is our peace

give us
this day
every day
bread for our
spiritual journey

forgive
as we forgive
let us
not fall
into temptation
or wander
into dangerous
places
without
your grace

deliver us
from evil
and from
the great deception
that it
doesn't exist

Father
bring us
into your presence
help us
to live worthily
the new life
You give us

Rev. Peter L. Chabot, M.M.

The Virgin of Smolensk
Anonymous
(10th Century Russian Icon)

a basic
description
of prayer
is the
raising of the mind
and heart
to God

there are many
methods
on how to pray
try them
pick a few
that work
for you

experience
the ways
and fruits
of prayer
by praying

a Russian peasant
tired of sermons
on prayer
came upon
the Jesus Prayer
where you
just keep saying

Lord Jesus Christ
Son of God
have mercy

therein he
finally found
constant

peace of heart
and food
for his soul

there are
many books
on prayer
but unless
they introduce one
to a life
of prayer
not just
saying
a few prayers
now and then
it is like
being
on the outside
looking in

o Lord
help me
bring into
my life
a habit
of prayer

leading
to growth
in holiness
and union
with You

Madonna and Child

Anonymous (Russian Mosaic)

there is an
instinctive
turning to God
in times
of great need
or difficulty
when awesome
things happen

a tidal wave
a volcanic
eruption

a magnificent
sunset
moments of pain
of joy
of sorrow
are inward
turning places
to meet the God

who created us
who loves us
who awaits us

the final chapters
of Job
offer a
reverent reflection
as God
poses questions
that are beyond
human ability
to answer

where were you
when I placed
the foundations
of the earth
and set a limit
to the sea

have you ever
called forth
the morning
have you measured
the plains
where
does light dwell
from whence
comes darkness

you must know
for you
were born
before them
and your days
are great

o Lord
grant me
your wisdom
grant me
your peace

Rev. Peter L. Chabot, M.M.

Virgin and Child
Jacopo da Sellaio
1441-1493

A traveler
to the
Holy Land
found a coin
from
New Testament times
bearing an
inscription
of the
Roman Legion
(these are now
under glass
in museums)

praying
the Rosary
mysteries
makes one
present to
that experience
in a much more
meaningful
and personal way
intervening
years fade away
like morning mist
we are there
at the Annunciation
accompany
Mary and Joseph
to Bethlehem
present also
as Jesus
begins
His ministry
mingle

with the guests
at Cana
see the raising
of Lazarus
partake
of the loaves
and fishes
are present at
the Last Supper
follow Our Lord
carrying
His Cross
behold Him
crucified
experience
the Resurrection
Pentecost

through this
meditative
and prayerful
journey
into the
world of the
Gospel
we become
more and more
conformed
to Jesus Christ

o Mother Mary
as your true
children
we ask you
to help us
on this journey

The Virgin and Child
Quentin Massys
1466–1536

devout
persevering prayer
health of soul
the favor of God
are attained
through devotion
to the Rosary
(Pope Leo XIII)

it is
a most effective
way to present
the chief mysteries
of our faith
a straight
and sure path
to God

these truths
are brought
before our minds
for contemplation
and raise
our minds
and hearts
in prayer

the Creed
becomes
more vital
in our lives
a fountain
of truth
in midst
of much error
strength

for our
human frailty

our most
basic relationship
to God
is revealed
in the
Our Father
the Hail Mary
asks our
Blessed Mother
for her help
now
and at the
hour
of our death
the Gloria
hymn of praise

the Rosary
can be a part
of our journey
of faith
as every day
brings us closer
to judgment

and
as we hope
and pray
to
eternal life

Rev. Peter L. Chabot, M.M.

The Virgin and Child
Parmigianino
1503-1540

sport teams
are geared
not for
just
one game
but for
a season

first there is
training
working on
the basics

keeping
in shape
conferences
lectures
watching film
learning
how to do it
practice
practice
and
more practice

then come
exhibition games
what went right
what went wrong
repeating essentials
until reaction
replaces
just thinking
about
what to do
working on

special situations

the spiritual
life
follows
the same routine

looking at
a whole
season
not just
a single game

learning
the basics
applying them
over and over

looking
at flaws
in an effort
to reduce them

working
as a team
as the Church
as the
Mystical Body
of Christ

please Lord
help us to
keep in training
and reach
our goal

Madonna and Child
Giovanni Bellini
1459-1516

two different
kinds of groups
visit
the Holy Land
pilgrims
and tourists

the tourist
goes to get
a vacation
experience

the pilgrim
is looking for
something
else

found only
on a journey
of faith
measured by
an entirely
different standard

the benefits gained
are interior
the journey
mainly spiritual

the sites and scenes
of the Holy Land
take on
another meaning

names and places
Nazareth
Bethlehem
Capharnaum
Jerusalem
evoke feelings
of reverence

a bygone era
becomes current
and familiar

an interior
expansion
opens on to
the timeless vista
of one's
unchanging
homeland
a return
of the soul
to a place
of rest
and refreshment

summer breezes
still sway
lilies of the
fields there
sunlight
unendingly shines
on the
Sea of Galilee

Jesus himself
greets us
with His peace

we are home

Rev. Peter L. Chabot, M.M.

Madonna of the Stars
Jacopo Tintoretto
1518-1594

i once stood
on the beach
of an island
in the Caribbean
and imagined
the world
of pirates
buccaneers
and the
huge amount
of plunder
still sunken there

the violent
outcome
of those who
had gained
and lost
in bloody
and hotly
contested battles
now lost
and forgotten

treasures
whose whereabouts
if known
would set off
another cycle
of furtive
and deadly
attempts
to gain
these fleeting
and slippery

riches
and doomed
to the
same end
like winged
insects
attracted to
and perishing
in a candle
flame

how different
are spiritual
treasures
those stored up
in heaven
imperishable
gaining interest
through
all eternity
gilt edged
securities
forever held
always
at hand
reversing
the popular
refrain

yes
yes you can
take it
with you

Madonna and Child with Angels
Antonio da Correggio
1489-1516

Some big time
lottery winners
were interviewed
years later

for
most of them
it would
have been
better
not to
have won
all that
money

marriages
broke up
long lost
so called friends
and relatives
started
showing up

sure fire deals
requiring loans
materialized
out of
nowhere

and the money
started to
disappear
like water
running down
the drain

harassment
resentment
no one
satisfied
with whatever
they were able
to pry loose
from the
windfall
a smoldering
dissatisfaction
with the
whole experience
and a lot of
expensive tastes

Lord
help me
to seek
and to find
spiritual riches
the only ones
that
really last

Rev. Peter L. Chabot, M.M.

The Holy Family with St. Anne
Jacob Jordaens
1593-1678

God
is present
within us

you are
temples of God
and the Holy Spirit
dwells within you

God is with us
in prayer

where two
or three
are gathered
in my name
I am with them

to comfort
enlighten
strengthen
pardon
protect

in times of
trial
temptation
suffering as
light in darkness
strength
in our weakness
guidance
nourishment

God is
especially present
in Jesus

his Son
and happy
are we
if we can
pronounce
his name
in faith
for no one
can say
Jesus is Lord
except
in the Holy
Spirit

let us then
often speak
his Holy Name
with reverence
and confidence
that the Lord
may accompany
us here
lead us
to our true home
that we may
continue
to profess
his name
in thanksgiving
and praise
throughout
the endless ages
of eternity

The Virgin with Grapes
Pierre Mignard
1610 - 1695

our
Blessed Mother
figures
prominently
in Old Testament
prophecies

she is there
from the
beginning
as the
New Eve
mother of the
new creation
she is the
chosen instrument
by whom
God will send
the Messiah
his Son
to redeem
a fallen
world

the chosen
people of old
had the Ark
of the Covenant
containing
tablets
of the law
and manna
on their journeys

Mary is
the new Ark
of the new
Covenant
carrying
bringing forth
the true
life-giving
bread
from heaven
for the
life of the world
with the
promise
of life forever
she is mother
in God's family
she is queen
of God's kingdom
for what
is a family
without a mother
or a kingdom
without a queen

she is
our hope
that with her
guidance
love
and care
her wandering
children
may find
their way home

Rev. Peter L. Chabot, M.M.

Madonna and Child with Saints
Andrea Mantegna
1489-1534

like three
sturdy legs
of a stool
the Church's
ancient practice
of prayer
fasting
and almsgiving
provide
an effective
plan
a proven means
to integrate
the spiritual
dimensions
in one's own life

prayer
is the oxygen
needed
to breathe in
spiritual strength
fasting
mental and physical
bars what is
harmful
almsgiving
provides outreach
to others

however
each in isolation
is vulnerable
prayer alone
can become

an exercise
of isolated
self-absorption
fasting
could become a
stoic approach
to life
almsgiving
done more to
promote oneself
than to
help others

they need to be
integrated
imbued with
Gospel values
to insure
being carried out
in the proper manner
and to bear
their promised
fruit
a maturing
life with God
here
and hereafter

Madonna Worshiping the Child
Biagio d'Antonio
1446-1516

faith
is not just
intellectual
assent
but a way
of life

living by
relying on
totally
confiding in
Jesus Christ
God's only Son
and living this
new life
he brings us
as children
of God

unlike
merely human life
constantly
under fire
by the prospect
of calamities
and uncertainty

the faith life
is grounded
in God
and backed up
by the promise
of whatever
we need
and ask for
will be provided

these prayers
are always
answered
although
the manner
may come
as a surprise
unexpectedly
in disguise
on a deeper level
than that for
which we
had asked

the doorway
to this
Gospel world
in and
around us
is opened

by faith
let us pray
for a strong
faith
and a deep
prayer life
to sustain it

Rev. Peter L. Chabot, M.M.

The Immaculate of El Escorial
Bartolome Esteban Murillo
1617-1683

An old time
freighter
bound for
South America
following its
compass heading
nearly
ran aground
in heavy fog

the compass
had been hung
near a
large iron spike
that distorted it
pulling the
needle away
from its
true heading

the same thing
can happen
in life

true meaning
and direction
can be pulled away
by allurements
and attractions
of the world
and end up
in shipwreck

our Lord
tells us
I am the way

in union
with Him
i still live
my human life
but it is now
a life of faith
in the Son of God
who loved me
and gave Himself up
for me

this life
we begin
here and now
is the same one
we hope to live
in its plentitude
and fullness
throughout
eternity

Lord Jesus
keep us
on course
and united to You
on our journey

Immaculate of the Crescent Moon
Bartolome Esteban Murillo
1617-1682

peace…

what a
beautiful gift
that everyone
seeks
but only a few
find
because it is
looked for
in the wrong
places

God's peace
is not a mere
cessation
of hostilities
but a blessed
calming
of the
deep anxieties
of the human spirit
filling it
with the balm
of divine consolation

only God
can grant this
and therefore
it is only
to be found
in God
through his Son
the Prince
of Peace

the shallow waters
of worldly peace
are easily
muddied
worldly peace
is fragile
slips away
at the slightest
provocation

there is nothing
substantial
to guarantee
it will hold up

God's peace
is deep
and unshakable
meets trouble
head-on
sticks around
carries one
on through
whatever storms
may continue
to rage

Lord
give us
your peace
the abiding
sustaining
comfort
of your peace

Rev. Peter L. Chabot, M.M.

The Nativity After 1525
Bernardino Luini
1480-1532

a book
on recent
history
carried the
evocative title
Only Yesterday
perfectly
setting mood
and atmosphere
for its perusal

we could say
the same
for the Gospels
written
only yesterday
for the events
described are
as new and fresh
and life-giving
today
as then

the doorway
into this world
is opened
by faith
sustained
by prayer
and sacrament

the events described
have the
same relevance
they had then
for at their center
is Jesus Christ

the Son of God
the same
yesterday
today and forever

speaking
the same words
as then
words
of light
and peace and
power
able to reach
into the innermost
recesses of our
souls
and bring
healing
forgiveness
and that
wonderful feeling
of being able
to start anew
no matter what

Lord
help us
to hear and heed
your word
that we may
today also
join that
blessed company
whose lives
were changed
and transformed
only yesterday

32

Adoration of the Shepherds
Bronze Doors at St. John the
Divine, New York
Henry Wilson
1864-1932

pilgrims from
all nations
come to
Jerusalem
during
Holy Week

there is a
public
Way of the Cross
through
the streets
part of the
continual
playing out
of the
central drama
of the human race

redemption
by the
Son of God
coming here
dying
rising again
that we might have
new life

most of the original
Station sites
are covered
by the rubble
of centuries
but here and there
some are
rightly marked

as are
the places
of his
Crucifixion
and burial

a few flagstones
upon which
our Lord stood
have been
uncovered

people of faith
stand out
you can see it
in their eyes
and reverent
demeanor
their presence
still bringing
comfort
to our Lord
helping him
to carry his Cross
with their
compassionate
meditation
and
o wondrous exchange
as He in turn
helps them
carry theirs

Rev. Peter L. Chabot, M.M.

Virgin and Child with Saints
Boccaccio Boccaccino
1446-1516

the Magnificat
of our Lady
is a way of life
a pathway
a set of attitudes
for true
happiness

it proclaims
in joyful praise
that only God
is great

all other
greatness
derives from Him
thus escaping
the prison
of isolated self
locked in
self-absorption
and human
limitation

in God
we find mercy
and divine
strength

the mighty
in their own
estimation
are left in
confusion
while the
lowly

the humble
walk
in the presence
of God
and dwell
in his courts

He fills
the hungry
while the rich
in their own
consideration
go hungry
filled only
with themselves
and are left
barren and
desolate

while those
who seek God
are given
the peace
and joy
of the promise
made to
Abraham
and his
descendants

forever

The Adoration of the Shepherds
Jan Cossiers
1600-1671

true peace
is rare
much of
the news
and even
entertainment
have a
heaviness
about them
offering little
to lift
the spirits

there is a
huge difference
between
worldly peace
and
that described
in the Gospel

when
our Lord says
my peace
I give you
not
as the world
gives
He is speaking
of a gift
of the Holy Spirit

a psalm
tells us
to seek
and strive

after peace
the peace
that comes
from God

send
upon us
o Lord
the gift
of true peace
so that
we may
more and more
seek You
the Giver
of every
good gift

that these
may be
a pledge
and prelude
to eternal life
and
eternal peace

Rev. Peter L. Chabot, M.M.

Gebert Christi
Lorenzo di Credi
1459-1537

Flying
in a
small plane
one seems
freed from
the bond
of earth's
gravity

rising
for the moment
above
this limitation

quilted
farm lands
lie below
you fly
through clouds
that
you can
reach out
and touch

you see
the beginning
and the end
of a train at a
railroad crossing
while below
there is an
interminable
wait

a pale blue sky
meets earth's
curving rim

beyond
endless space

you arrive
at your destination
faster
the scenic beauty
is magnificent

and when a
tropical storm
bounces
the plane around
like a ping pong ball
and heavy rain
beats against
frail fabric
and
visibility is
zero

then
you trust
your instruments
to maintain
direction
and level flight

the teaching
of the Church
is like
these instruments

the whole
experience like
the adventure
of faith

36

Glory to God
Kim Ki-chang
1914-2001

how much
should i pray

a farmer
had a bull
that fell
into an
open pit

there was
no way
to get it out

no crane
in the county
was
big enough
nor
could he
strap on
a lifting harness
without being
severely
injured

over near
the barn
was a pile
of sand

the farmer
began filling
a wheelbarrow
and dumping it
into the pit
slowly bringing
the level

to where
the bull
could scramble out
by filling
all maneuverable
space with sand

the same
can be done
to rid one
of habits of sin
addiction
depression
despair

crowd these out
with prayer
spiritual reading
good works

leaving them
no space
to inflict
their damage

while at the
same time
building
a strong
spiritual foundation
able to take on
and overcome
whatever
might try
to bring it down

Rev. Peter L. Chabot, M.M.

Adoration of the Magi
Sandro Botticelli
1444-1510

prayer
has been
called
the language
of faith
but
one needs
to speak
a language
or it falls
into disuse

it requires
lifelong
application

there are
many ways
of praying

alone
in community
mentally
vocally
in silence
with
or without
written material

there are
different kinds
of prayer

prayer books
novenas
litanies
the Rosary

way of the Cross
the Jesus prayer
prayers of
praise
petition
adoration
contrition
thanksgiving
short aspirations
spontaneous

but the
basics
of prayer
remain
the same

a lifting
of the mind
and heart
to God
in faith
hope
and love

Lord
teach us
to pray
give us
the spirit
of prayer
to pray well
to pray often

Adoration of the Magi
Hieronymus Bosch
1450-1516

revelation
reveals to us
who God is

it also reveals
who we are

Jesus uses
fire
as a symbol
of our transformation
into children
of God

and
we become
temples
of the Holy Spirit
sons and
daughters of God
by adoption
what Jesus is
by nature

fires lit
by lightning
among the
giant Sequoia
burn away
surface growth
and provide
the right conditions
for new growth
to appear

a forest fire
is a vivid reminder
of the
four last things
death judgment
heaven hell

but
fire also
provides warmth
and light

a votive light
telling of
the Lord's presence
in the
Blessed Sacrament
enchants
attracts
invites

o Holy Spirit
you came
in tongues of fire
at Pentecost

come now
and enkindle
in our souls
the fire
of thy love

Rev. Peter L. Chabot, M.M.

The Flight into Egypt
Fra Angelico
1387-1455

salvation
doesn't refer only
to future
beatitude

its benefits
begin now

there is
salvation
from ignorance
of the meaning
and purpose
of life

salvation
brings
the gifts
of the
Holy Spirit

faith hope
love joy
peace
self-control

and the grace
and power
to make them
come alive

salvation
bestows
a created
participation

in God's
own life
making us
his children

this is
a new life
and the
assistance
needed
to live it

salvation
brings freedom
from bondage
to sin and evil
frees us
from their
dominion

the most basic
and important
of all
freedoms

grant us
o Lord
your salvation

The Flight into Egypt
Joachim Patinir
1480–1524

The
Hail Mary
has a special
efficacy
in asking
our Lady's
help and
intercession

the Rosary
hymns
in her praise
litanies
prayed slowly
and reflectively

contain a
wealth of
meditational
and devotional
resources
to help
stay focused
and reduce
distraction

the Holy Names
bring us
into the presence
of Jesus
and Mary

they are
a shield
against temptation
give direction

guidance
spiritual joy
in a world
of false pleasures
that lead
to guilt
and remorse

they bring
the clarity
of truth
in the midst
of so much
delusion

fulfillment
in place of
emptiness

a beginning
of that
peace and
happiness
we hope
to enjoy
throughout
the endless
ages
of eternity

Rev. Peter L. Chabot, M.M.

The Rest on the Flight into Egypt
Gerard Davis
1460-1523

great enterprises
projects
of magnitude
have simple
beginnings
they grow
in the course
of time
to assume
proportions
that can
be daunting
to those
who wish
to follow
similar pursuits

but
like in
out of the way
mountain areas
where a bridge
is needed
to cross
a chasm
or a
rushing river
a single cord
is flown
to the other side
by kite
or tied
to an arrow

once this
is secured
a stronger cord

is tied to this
and pulled across

then a rope
then a larger one
in like manner
til one
thick enough
to form
a foundation
for a rope bridge
is in place
then
one by one
others are
added
and the
end result
is a combination
of many
smaller efforts

so too
in the spiritual life
patient
and persevering
work
at building
a prayer life
a cord
a strand
a rope
at a time
builds
a solid bridge
to God

Repose in Egypt
Bernard Plockhorst
1820-1907

a few
of the qualities
needed
in prayer
are
that it be
trusting

whatever
you ask for
believe
and it shall
come to you

persevering

ask
and keep on asking
seek
and keep on seeking
knock
and keep on knocking

humble

the Lord
resists the proud
and gives grace
to the humble

continuing

as we need
daily vitamins
and nourishment
so too
in a regular
manner

do we need
spiritual
nourishment

prayers
are always
answered
sometimes
in surprising
ways

at other times
by instilling
a habit
of prayer
through constant
practice

because
a spirit
of prayer
is one of
God's greatest
gifts
an ever present
means at hand
to obtain
the graces
and helps
we need
with the surety
of receiving
them

Rev. Peter L. Chabot, M.M.

Madonna with Saints Adoring the Child
Pietro Peragino
1446-1524

I in the
early days
of photography
images
only remained
a short time
then they
faded
and became
unrecognizable

there had to
be a way
to hold
the image
to make
it permanent

there was
a need for
a solution
that would fix
the photo
and let it
not grow dim

the same
holds true
when one
starts on the spiritual
journey

a way
must be found
to keep it
from fading
a few prayers

only now and then
will fade away
as other cares
move in

a New York
cab driver
supplied
the missing
element
when asked
by a tourist
how to get to
Carnegie Hall
half turned
and said slowly
and distinctly

practice
practice
practice

the indispensable
irreplaceable
and necessary
component
of any
serious enterprise

o Lord
instill in us
the habit
of prayer
a constant
persistent
persevering
habit of prayer

Madonna della Purity
Luis de Morales
1510-1586

when
King Richard
was captured
during the time
of the Crusades

he was imprisoned
held for ransom
no one
knew where
he was

his court
musician
journeyed by
horseback
past castles
and places
of confinement
singing ballads
and songs
of Richard's homeland
tirelessly
he did this
and for some time
finally
passing by a castle
faintly at first
then
stronger
he was joined
by a voice
coming from
a dungeon within
the balladier

stopped
tears came to
his eyes
he had found
the king

the Holy Spirit
sings to us
songs
of our
true homeland
stirring words
and melodies
songs
for our pilgrim
journey
songs of our
real and lasting
home
with God

come Holy Spirit
guide us
on our way
or on our way back
into your
presence
to find
our only
true rest
true peace
at last
only here

Rev. Peter L. Chabot, M.M.

Madonna in Glory with Child and Saints
Pietro Peragino
1446-1524

the Beatitudes
and the
first Psalm
start out
with the word
blessed
happy
the one who
follows
these ways
happiness
is within
their context

Cyprus
has been called
the happy isle
the same adjective
as used
in the
Beatitudes

the island provides
everything
needed
for the sustenance
of life
many crops
grow in
abundance

the climate
is pleasant
there are
plenty of
natural resources

the island
is well situated
for commerce

the Beatitudes
could also
be called
a happy island
supplying
what is needed
for the spiritual life

the way of life
outlined
in the Beatitudes
becomes clearer
when set against
their opposites

poor in spirit
instead of selfish
proud arrogant
those who mourn
are compassionate
not frivolous
self-centered
the meek
are even tempered
versus the
overbearing

the persecuted
who have something
worth dying for
but especially
worth
living for

Madonna with Child
Pietro Peragino
1446-1524

the Archbishop
ascended into
the pulpit
to relate
a remarkable
conversion story

years ago
a young man
he knew
was dared
to make a
mock confession
which he did

but added
to the gravity
of this
by directing
a taunting
reproach
to the Crucifix

yet the holy prelate
kept referring
to God's mercy
perhaps
the congregation
thought
just perhaps
as a young priest
the archbishop
was called
for a deathbed
repentance
to some

miserable hovel
where
wasted by
disease
this pitiful
individual
lay dying

perhaps
you are wondering
he continued
if he was given
a second chance
even
to start anew
to make amends

and I tell you
yes
yes he was
one that
took his
breath away
one he
would never
have dared
to hope for
or dream of

for you see
he said

i am
that man

Rev. Peter L. Chabot, M.M.

The Madonna in Majesty
Giovanni Cimabue
1242-1302

there are
two kingdoms
each vying
for an allegiance
that is total
brooking
no compromise
accepting
no concessions
there is
no middle ground

the kingdom
of God calls for
complete
and total
dedication
to its cause
and its leader
this is the most
powerful kingdom
the other
has been
vanquished
once
and for all

on the summit
of Calvary
Jesus
released us
from the bondage
of sin
and He has
set us free

from its
degrading
and oppressive
tyranny
brought us
into
the exhilarating
realm
and reality
of being
children of God

from
his empty tomb
we hear
the hollow echo
of the once feared
and fearful
call of death
vanquished forever
by the might
of his Resurrection

let us go forth then
with and in Christ
and enter into
the final stage
of his kingdom

Madonna Col Bambino
Sebastiano Mainardi
1460-1513

a spiritual classic
the practice
of the
presence of God
takes the name
Emmanuel
God with us
literally

Brother Lawrence
lived out
this reality
daily witnessing
the truth
of the presence
of God
in whom we live
and move
and have
our being

God with us
at the beginning of
St. Matthew
and affirmed
at its close
behold
I am with you
all days
till the end
of the age

he took
this teaching
to heart
and became
a living example
of what happens
when we
really believe
this amazing
Gospel truth

the Lord
is with us
in the Eucharist
in our hearts
in prayer
in our neighbor

in moments of
inspiration
invitations
to draw closer
live in
deeper union
with the One
who alone
can satisfy
the deepest yearning
of the human soul

come Lord Jesus
come into our
hearts
make your
presence known
may You be
the guide
the inspiration
and nourishment
on our
life's journey

Rev. Peter L. Chabot, M.M.

Virgin Annunciate
Antonello da Messina
1430–1479

The Blessed
Virgin Mary
has a unique
and exalted
relationship
with the
Most Holy
Trinity

beloved daughter
of the Father
spouse
of the
Holy Spirit
mother
of the Son

who
from the Cross
gave her
to us
and us
to her
as our mother

a proven
means to a
deeper
relationship
with Jesus
and Mary
is the Rosary

a favored
prayer
of saints
and holy people

it became
a lifeline
for Bishop Walsh
during
twelve years
of imprisonment
providing all
he needed
when other means
were lacking
(he prayed
eighteen a day)

if we pray it
ourselves
with our families
it will provide
the same graces
we and our
weary world
need so much

our Lady
promises
that those
who pray it
will not be
overcome by
misfortune
or die
a bad death

which is
in effect
a promise
of eternal life

Poliptych of Perugia
Piero della Francesca
1415-1492

repent
for the kingdom
of God
is at hand

this kingdom
has three aspects

first
there is the
kingdom within
wherein
values
goals
a code of conduct
and one's
entire life
are arranged
according
to certain
standards
the kingdom within
accepts
and makes welcome
the reign of God
in our lives
by a life of faith
not just
intellectual belief
but a
confiding in
living by
relying on God
in all things
and in all
circumstances

there is
a social aspect
a living out
in community
the dictates
and mode
of being
as citizens
of that kingdom
where
the duties and
their exercise
are evident
in one's life

then there is
the final aspect

the kingdom
to come
in its fullness
of peace
and joy
with God
in company
of all the saints
through
all the
endless days
of eternity

Rev. Peter L. Chabot, M.M.

Annunciation
Fra Filippo Lippi
1406-1469

two men
were playing golf
look
one said
i'm doing fine
business
is great

what can i
do for you

well uh
responded
the other
i could use
a couple of
golf clubs

a few
days later
he received
an e-mail

i just
bought you
four golf clubs

three have
dining facilities

the fourth
has an
indoor pool
and a
driving range

have a
nice day

God's response
to prayer
overwhelms
our wildest
expectations
the effects
and results
of prayer
go way beyond
what we expect
or pray for

Lord
help us
to pray more
to bring
a prayerful spirit
into our lives

Annunciation
Fra Filippo Lippi
1406-1469

there is
an inner
yearning
to excel
to go beyond
the ordinary
that
when blocked
or not followed
brings frustration

in a classic
stage play
*On the
Waterfront*
Marlon Brando
plays
a boxer
who has
to throw
a fight

i coulda
had class
he laments
i coulda
been a contenda
i coulda been
somebody

on a
much higher
level
we are all
called

to go beyond
the ordinary
to fulfill
a supernatural
destiny
to become
children
of God

St. Augustine
says
You have
created us
for Yourself
o God
and our hearts
are restless
until they
rest
in Thee

grant us
o Lord
the grace
to hear
and answer
your call

Rev. Peter L. Chabot, M.M.

The Annunciation
Sandro Botticelli
1445-1510

a woman
was walking
along an English
shore line

it started
to rain
became heavier
there was
a cottage
nearby
so she
sought refuge
under the
roof of
a small porch
and knocked

the door
opened
and she asked
if perhaps
she might
borrow
an umbrella
which would
be returned
the following day
the householder
had two
umbrellas
one almost new
the other
badly
in need
of repair

this one
was given
to the woman
standing outside
for she had
not been invited in

the next day
a royal carriage
pulled up
in front of
the cottage

the coachman
knocked at
the door

Her Majesty
thanks you
for the use
of the umbrella

Her Majesty?

yes
Queen Victoria

of all sad words
of tongue or pen
the saddest are these
it might have been

and yet this is much
the way
our Blessed Mother
is treated today

Annunciation
Tiziano Vecelli (Titian)
1473-1576

why are
you so sad
Blessed Mother
why are
you weeping
why do
your statues
shed tears

because of you
my children
because you
do not pray
you do not
take my messages
to heart

because so many
of you are being
swept away
led astray by
the evil one

because so many
are falling
into hell
because there is
no one to pray
for them

listen
to my pleas
my beloved
children
stop sinning
stop committing
sin

return to God
who loves you
so much
return to Jesus
who redeemed you

pray
pray
pray the Rosary
sacrifice
do penance

pray much
pray often
and
do not
lose heart

in the end
my Immaculate
Heart
will triumph

Lovely Lady
dressed in blue,
teach us
how to pray
God was just
your little boy
and you know
the way

Rev. Peter L. Chabot, M.M.

Annunciation
Leonardo da Vinci
1452-1519

major shipping
ports
send local
harbor pilots
out to meet
docking ships

their expertise
in safe procedures
guides the vessels
to their
proper berths

hidden reefs
and sunken wrecks
lie in wait
for the
unwary

traffic lanes
in tight spaces
need to be
followed
exactly
to avoid
collision

papers
and reports
need to be
filled out
latest rules
explained
the older and more
experienced
the sea captains

the more
they appreciate
this service
and its value

Jesus Christ
is both our
sea captain
and harbor pilot
on life's voyage
He alone
insures a
good crossing
and happy
ending
helping us
traverse
the last great
barrier reef
of death

He leads
and guides us
past the
dangerous rip tides
treacherous
cross currents
and safely
on into
the fair harbors
of eternal life

Early Morning Meditations

Virgin of Humility
Jacopo Bellini
1400-1470

during the
French Revolution
some nuns
were brought
to the guillotine
like so many
sheep led
to slaughter

Mother Superior
had told them
if any chose
to leave
they had permission

some did

a horse drawn cart
pulled away
from the convent
took them
to the instrument
of death
outlined starkly
against a
brooding sky
midst a
cacophony
of insults
and blasphemies

but even
this hostile crowd
became silent
as the sisters
in solemn

single file
ascended the steps
singing
their evening
vesper song

the sound
diminished
and finally ended
by a blood soaked
blade

but
the final phrase
was taken up
by the youngest
hitherto
hidden
in the crowd

once more
the heavy
dreadful knife
was raised
and dropped
again

they waited
smiling
at the entrance
to eternity
while she
hurried
to catch up
with them

Rev. Peter L. Chabot, M.M.

Annunciation
Sandro Botticelli
1445-1510

standing firm
endurance
patience
perseverance
are necessary
qualities
in the spiritual combat

but a
voluntary acceptance
of spiritual hardship
as a means of
strengthening
and purifying
faith

a resource
and refuge
in times of
painful situations
opposition
criticism
privation
persecution
physical and
moral ailments
aridity
weariness

a building
of toughness
into the fabric
of the spiritual life
a reserve
of strength
for hard times
and the difficult task
of atonement for sin
they are necessary
to follow
in the footsteps
of Jesus

standing firm
endurance
patience
perseverance

in our own
way of the cross

keys to
spiritual equanimity
in midst of
storms within
tempests without

they are a
necessary means
for a closer
union with God

take up
your cross
and follow Me

they are not a
stoic resignation
to something
we cannot change
or escape

The Annunciation
Paolo de Matteis
1662-1728

blessed
are the meek

a problem
with the word meek
is that it
connotes timidity
which is
far from its
true meaning

Moses is
described as
being meek
so there must be
a lot more
to it

meekness here
means being
in control
of oneself
not being
carried away
by the passions

having
poise
composure
approachability
mildness
patience

it is one of the
gifts of
the Holy Spirit

recall a rodeo
the gate opens
an angry bull
comes exploding
out of the pen
with a cowboy
perched precariously
on top
hanging on
for dear life
if he stays there
for eight seconds
he gets a prize

sometimes
he actually
tames the bull
till it slows down
and walks around

the cowboy
is a good example
of biblical meekness

one tough hombre

Father
grant us
the gifts
of the Holy Spirit
that are for
our happiness
and fulfillment

Rev. Peter L. Chabot, M.M.

The Black Madonna of Czestochowa
Anonymous (14th Century)

An inheritance
or trust fund
sufficient to
provide for
every need
is something
relatively few
can look
forward to

there is another
inheritance
and trust fund
on a much
higher plane
available
to all
it is a birthright
given through
Baptism
that makes us
sons and daughters
of Almighty God

it provides
freedom
from bondage
to sin
and its eternal
consequences
it brings us
here and now
the divine gifts
of the Holy Spirit

it gives us
new life

spiritual
nourishment

when
temporal wealth
drops
in value
heaven's
increases

when
worldly riches
fall prey
to the spoilage
of time
loss
thievery

heaven's
inheritance
keeps on
accruing
interest
and dividends

Lord
we give thanks
for the security
afforded us
from your bounty
help us
to use it well
that it might
gain for us
eternal life

Assumption of the Virgin
Antonio de Correggio
1489-1534

the annals
of sailing history
tell of
a ship
far from home port
that was sinking

another
happening by
came to offer
assistance
but
too much water
had come in
the troubled
vessel sank
leaving crew
and passengers
struggling
to stay afloat
in the middle
of nowhere

the other ship
was able
to crowd them
on board

then this ship
sprung a leak

but with
the extra hands
they were able
to stay afloat

until they
reached safety

we are called
to help
and support
one another
by prayer
and good works
that what
is lacking
in one
may be
complemented
by another

Lord
help us to see
each other
as brothers
and sisters
in the
family of God
helping
each other
on our journey
into your kingdom

Rev. Peter L. Chabot, M.M.

Assumption of the Virgin
Annibale Carracci
1560-1609

T

the Holy Sacrifice
of the Mass
is a re-presentation
of the Last Supper
Passion Death
and Resurrection
of Jesus Christ
in the here and now

its origins
go back
into the Old
Testament
they find
their full
expression
and fulfillment
in the New

Passover
recalls the time
when an
avenging angel
passed over
houses sprinkled
with the blood
of a
sacrificed lamb
symbolizing Christ
pouring out
his Blood
for our salvation
and becoming
the New
Paschal Lamb

manna would

become
Living Bread
come down
from heaven

Jesus changes
water into wine
at Cana

later
He will
change wine
into his Blood
with a
separate consecration
and a breaking
of the Host
signifying
his sacrificial
death
on the Cross

many grains
are ground into
one bread
many grapes
crushed
into one wine
showing
that through
many trials
we who
are made one
are made one
in the Mystical Body
of Christ

Coronation of the Virgin
Diego Velasquez
1599-1660

only in God
is my soul
at rest
much of
what the world
sees as rest
is only
momentary escape
from life's troubles
and the
hectic travelling
there and back
is no help

more likely
than not
we bring our
problems
and preoccupations
with us
ending up
just as tired
and hassled
as before
nor do the
agencies
ever mention
the mosquitoes

resting in God
is of a
different kind
and quality
it brings about
true rest
true peace

both restorative
and refreshing

come to Me
all you who labor
and are
heavily burdened
and I will
give you rest

take up your cross
and follow me
for paradoxically
only by accepting
the cross
do we find rest
because Jesus himself
helps us
carry it and
it thus becomes
a means of
grace
peace
rest

o blessed burden
writes St. Bernard
that makes
all burdens
light

Rev. Peter L. Chabot, M.M.

Madonna with Christ Child and St. Francis
Titiano Vecelli (Titian)
1473-1576

the central
teaching of
St. John
of the Cross
is the essence
of simplicity

the Blessed Trinity
dwells within
is reached
along an
interior road
devoid
of any
attachment
that is not
of God

like a log
placed in a
fireplace

popping
snapping
crackling
as all
unfitness
is burned away
there is left
only a
quiet slow
dance of flame
from a
glowing ember

sustained
and maintained
in and by
the fire itself

a place
and scene
of enchanting
beauty
and restful
peace

where the soul
partakes
of divinity

as Jesus
partakes of
our humanity

and we become
by adoption
true children
of God

sons and
daughters
of
the Most High

Early Morning Meditations

Virgin of the Navigators
Alejo Fernandez
1475-1545

some metals
have a magnetic
force within
that can
attract objects

these are
relatively weak

but if a
magnet
of soft iron
is surrounded
by a coil
of copper wire
and an
electric current
is passed
through it
an electromagnet
of surprising
force and
possibilities
results

in like manner
grace added to
human efforts
enables that
which
human nature
by itself
cannot accomplish

raised
on eagle's wings
it attains
the impossible

but
remains humble
in the
realization
of how
it got there

dear Lord
transform
our lives
with
your grace
your presence

make us
worthy of
eternal life

Rev. Peter L. Chabot, M.M.

Trivulzio Madonna
Andrea Mantegna
1431–1506

I
in the
New Testament
world
where Jesus
established
his reign
and his kingdom
there were three
main languages
with seemingly
insurmountable
barriers
dividing them

Hebrew
the language
of religion

Latin
the language
of the law

Greek
the language
of philosophy

not only
different languages
but also
different alphabets

few could
read or speak
all three

national
social

and personal
conflicts
and antagonisms
were rife

how could
all this
ever be

reconciled

unified

brought to
fulfillment

on the
hill of Calvary
a Cross
is being raised

a tablet
proclaiming
the kingship
of Jesus Christ
is nailed
to this Cross

and the
inscription
is written

in Hebrew
in Latin
and in Greek

Madonna of the Rosary
Michaelangelo Merisi da
Caravaggio
1571–1610

on a
bleak
and overcast day
on Calvary
the prophecy
of Simeon
behold
a sword
shall pierce
thine own heart
was fulfilled

the deeper
the love
the more
intense
the suffering
one undergoes
in seeing
one loved
so afflicted
and no
human love
ever matched
our Lady's love
for her Son

so intense
her agony
in beholding
Jesus
in his
most cruel torment
that had not
grace intervened
her human
nature
could not
have borne it

her agony
was like his
for her
wandering
and lost
children
bequeathed
to her
by Jesus
on his Cross
her love
for them
also like his
deriving
from her
new title
Mother
of us all

Mother Mary
help us
to live
our lives
as your
true children
bring us
to where
you reign
as mother
and queen

Rev. Peter L. Chabot, M.M.

Madonna with the Child
Giovanni Bellini
1430-1516

the need
for the grace
of God
is manifest
in every
aspect
of our lives

unless
the Lord
watch over
the city
in vain
does the
watchman
keep vigil

even
the wish
to accomplish
something for God
is a special grace
an invitation
and ought
to be
a source
of consolation
that God
would
send to me
not just
a general call
but an rsvp

if we
disdain this

and forego
God's help
we fall
back on
that most
erratic
and untrustworthy
of supports

unaided
human resources
that in
times of trial
suffering
discouragement
betrayal
are found
to be sadly
lacking
and we are
left alone
like
Willie Loman
in Death
of a Salesman

out there
trying to
make a go of it
alone
with but a smile
and a shoeshine

Early Morning Meditations

Madonna and Child
Jacopo Bellini
1400-1470

the relationship
between
prayer
and meditation
is like that between
kindling
and a campfire

when the fire
burns low
add more kindling
and it becomes
fire also

so too
meditation
supports
and can
turn into
prayer
by thinking about
mulling over
a scripture text
a spiritual thought
until it
catches the fire
of prayer
even in times
of dryness

if nothing
seems to work
try writing

messages
prayers
scripture
quotes

writing reinforces
reading and
listening
and is a
big help
in overcoming
distractions
temptations
even for
chasing the blues
if done
in a slow
leisurely
concentrated way
letting the words
sink in
be absorbed
like the
medieval monks
of old
copying
manuscripts

and thus
becomes
a prayerful activity
in itself

Rev. Peter L. Chabot, M.M.

Madonna della Vallicella
Peter Paul Rubens
1577–1640

one good
method
of prayer
is to
consciously
place oneself
in the presence
of God
in whom
we live
and move
and have our being

select a reading
meditate
on this reflectively

then comes
prayer itself
a colloquy
a conversation
a dialogue
with God
with our Lord
with our
Blessed Mother

let
the inner ear
listen
the heart
speak
unburden
itself
be washed

at the fountain
be healed
of the wounds
of sin
be consoled
by divine
consolation
be rested
in this place
of divine refuge
be strengthened
now
and for
the days
to come

Virgin and Child
Nicolas Poussin
1594-1665

different people
watching
the same sunset
may be
filled with
similar wonder
at this
awesome
spectacle

the sun is not
divided
or diminished
but appears
in all
its splendor
to each
beholder

different individuals
may listen
to the
same concert
absorbing
being moved
by the
rhythmic flow
and movement
of the orchestral
strains

a single performance
draws many
into its realm
with no dilution

no division
no diminution

in receiving
the holy Eucharist
each person
receives
the Lord
in all
his power
and grandeur
and majesty

each experiences
his love
and peace
each is strengthened
and encouraged
to continue
a journey
on which
He is the way

Rev. Peter L. Chabot, M.M.

Virgin and Child with Infant St. John
Jan Bruegel the Younger
1601–1678

willing
acceptance
is the key
to the Christian
concept
of suffering

carrying
our cross
with Christ
on his
way of
the cross
that also
becomes ours

patient
endurance
is a key
attitude

all this
is not
stoic acceptance
or
grim forbearance
of something
we cannot
change
but would
if we could

joining
our Lord
on his way
brings union

meaning
and strength
to carry ours

to atone
for sin
to gain
for ourselves
and others
strength
to carry theirs

take
my yoke
upon you

and
you will
find rest
for your souls

Visitation
Domenico Ghirlandaio
1449-1494

the consequences
of sin
are
pain
suffering
hardship
alienation
from God
and finally
death

these are
the means
Jesus chose
to cancel
the humanly
unpayable debt
to restore
a fallen race
once again
to the
favor of God

and so
he assumed
our guilt
endured
unspeakable
pain
suffering
humiliation
even
the feeling
of alienation
from God

as
his life
is ours
so also
his way
of the cross
is ours

by accepting
suffering
in union with Jesus
we find peace
and life
with God

we help atone
for sin
erase guilt
and are
restored
to union
and friendship
with the Father

Rev. Peter L. Chabot, M.M.

Birth of the Virgin
Bartolome Esteban Murillo
1617-1682

boot camp
is a toughening
transforming
experience

instilling
Spirit
Tradition
Training

spirit
tradition
training

in the
formation of
prayer warriors
for the spiritual
combat
going on
within
and without

play a vital
role

survival techniques
weaponry
maneuvers
marching in step
physical
and mental
conditioning
studying
following maps
obstacle courses
live ammo
whizzing overhead

claiming
and receiving
a willing
and loyal
obedience
and adherence
to a Creed
and Practice
going back
to the Apostles

a spartan existence
focused on getting
combat ready
staying prepared

and passed on
as a sacred trust
and heritage
to succeeding
generations

the
Catholic faith
puts one through
a spiritual
boot camp

Flight into Egypt
Maurice Prendergast
1858-1924

happiness
blessedness
begins here
and gives
testimony
to one's being
on the sure path
leading to
eternal blessedness

it is a
special gift
of the Holy Spirit
making us partakers
of divinity
as Christ
partook
of our humanity

it brings
detachment
from false pleasures
helps us
seek and find
the true ones

this kind
of happiness
is independent
of what the world
can give
or take away

it sees us
through the pain
shines

through tears
not sought
in itself
but becomes a
by-product
of a way
of living

it is a
voluntary
poverty
not the kind
arising
from circumstance

to advance
in things above
we must be poor
in that which
drags us down
says St. Gregory

it is a
tranquil harbor
a treasure
laid up
in heaven

where your treasure is
there your heart will
be

Rev. Peter L. Chabot, M.M.

Flight into Egypt
Bartolome Esteban Murillo
1617-1682

the ways
of knowing God
are many
and varied

revelation
reason
creation

the teaching
and tradition
of the Church
the legacy
of the saints
our own
spiritual
journey

nature
mirrors God
science
ponders
his handiwork
wonder
attends
everything

even
the microscopic
world
has a marvelous
symmetry
and order

planet earth

traveling
awesomely

endlessly
unerringly
along
that narrow
and exceedingly
unique
and singular orbit
the one
and only place
in our galaxy
of a hundred
billion stars
where

life
is found
and flourishes

all this
and more
put the skeptic
in a position
more difficult
to justify
than the faith
he rejects

Adoration of the Shepherds
Sebastiano Ricci
1659-1734

I
if you are
risen with Christ
seek the things
that are above
from whence
come grace
power
wisdom
new life
freedom
from bondage to sin
and a worldly way
of living

all this
seems beyond
human capacity
and it is

without Me
you can do
nothing
our Lord
tells us

reliance on
human means only
is an impossible
massive obstacle
to this
new life
of grace

who will
take away
the stone
the women

asked themselves
on the way
to the tomb

and who
will take away
the stone
of our indifference
inertia
lethargy
in the
performance
of spiritual
duties
so as to
accomplish
our spiritual tasks

Lord
grant us
your divine help
for the work
You call us
to do
for the life
You call us
to live

Rev. Peter L. Chabot, M.M.

Madonna and Child
Jacopo Bellini
c.1400-c.1470

A a battleship
was on
maneuvers

foggy day
visibility
near zero

a bright light
appeared
dead ahead

an urgent
message
from the ship:

on a
collision course
change
your heading

a reply
cracked back:
change yours
immediately!

the captain
responded:
change your course
i'm a
battleship

the reply
(that ended
the argument
and sent

all hands
scrambling):

i'm a
lighthouse

God's will
is like
a lighthouse
there to
guide
and
to warn

to guide
along ways
that lead
to eternal life

to warn
against those
who plot
against it

Lord
help us
remember
that
only in
your will
is our safety
and our peace

Our Lady of Perpetual Help
Anonymous
15th Century

where is
the lamb

Isaac
asks
his father
Abraham

as he
climbs
the hill
carrying
wood
for the
sacrifice

God will provide
my son
Abraham
replies
overwhelmed
by grief
till
an angel
of the Lord
stays his hand

where is
the lamb
many ages
have asked
since then

where is He
the One
who will
pardon

our sins
remove
our guilt
heal
the rift
between
God and man

in the fullness
of time
John
the Baptist
on the
banks of
the Jordan
cries out:

Behold!
behold
the Lamb
of God

finally
here

finally
present
among us

Lamb of God
You take away
the sin
of the world
have mercy
on us

Rev. Peter L. Chabot, M.M.

Madonna and Child
Albrecht Durer
1471-1528

a fleet
of ships
was at
anchor
in the
Mediterranean
Sea

a fierce storm
arose

ships were all
pulled away
from their
anchorage
and dashed
to pieces
on the rocks

except one

it had
caught onto
an anchor
separated
from a
larger ship
on a previous
voyage

it was
larger
heavier
and buried
so deeply
it had
become
immovable

the smaller
ship's anchor
had attached
itself to the
larger one
and thus become
equally
immovable

united with
Jesus Christ
we borrow
from his
strength
receive
his protection

and likewise
become
immovable
when the
storms of
temptation
would drive us
to ruin

Lord
be my rock
my fortress
my strength
in all
the trials
of life

Madonna & Child & Ss. Martina And Agnes
El Greco
1541-1614

mine
cave-ins
are calamities
of the most
agonizing
kind

a group
of men
trapped
far below
the earth's surface

in darkness
no escape

a desperate
situation
with only
a glimmer
of hope
that a
rescue team
can reach them
before
it's too late

their sorrowing
families
huddled together
anxiously
intently
absorbing
each bit
of news

all humanity
before
the coming
of Christ
was in
the same
dire straits

a people
trapped
in darkness
sustained
only by hope
of deliverance
from outside

to fully
appreciate
the Incarnation
of Jesus Christ
into this world

it is needful to
remember
the darker times

Lord
grant us
grateful hearts
to thank You
for your coming

and prayerful
spirits
to keep it
meaningful

Rev. Peter L. Chabot, M.M.

Madonna and Child w/Ss. Jerome and John the Baptist
Cima da Conglio

distractions
in prayer
are a common
problem

one way
to diminish
them
is to hold
a word
or image
in mind
at various
points of
the prayer

like a
held note
in a musical
rendition

Hail Mary
full of grace
the Lord
is with thee

pause
recall
a scene
or the presence
of Jesus
and Mary

blessed
art thou
a lingering
emphasis
on blessed

pray
for us sinners

emphasize
and hold
for a moment
a picture
or holy card
may help
corral the
wandering
attention

and
focus it
on the prayer
to involve
the imagination
reflection
and will

Lord Jesus
teach us
to pray
grant us
the spirit
of prayer

Baby Jesus Sleeping
Benveneto Cellini
1500-1571

Ignace
Paderewski
composer
eminent
statesman
of Poland
during
the dark days
of World War II
gave hundreds
of immensely
popular concerts
to raise funds
to help his
beleaguered
nation

at one
of these
was a mother
with her
young son

momentarily
distracted
she looked
around and
his seat
was empty
he had
wandered up
onto the stage
lured by the
grand piano
shining
under the
spotlight

and begun
to play
a beginner's
tune
the audience
gasped
and directed
unfriendly glances
at the mother

at this moment
the maestro
appeared
approached
the piano
leaned over
and whispered

keep playing

stretched out
his arms
on either side
and added
an accompaniment
that raised
a simple tune
to high art

so keep on
playing

the Maestro
is accompanying
you

Rev. Peter L. Chabot, M.M.

Virgin of Humility
Jacopo Bellini
1400-1470

a common
occurrence with
prescribed
medicine
is to take it
until one
starts to
feel better
and then
stop

this can aggravate
the problem
because
no cure
is effected
during
too short
a time
of treatment
resistance
to the medicine
can build up
so that
it takes
a bigger dosage
next time

this also
occurs in the
spiritual life
treatment of
most ills
must be
continuous
and ongoing

building
strong defenses
to resist the
forces of evil

while at the
same time
attacking
the causes
whereby
defenses
were breached

Lord Jesus
come to
our aid
in our
continual need
for healing
and strength
in our
journey
to You
and
with You

Madonna
Biagio d'Antonio
1455–1510

I in
the Book
of Psalms
the word

selah

appears
frequently
it means

pause
and think
about this

in reading
scripture
and meditational
readings
it is a
good idea
to incorporate
frequent pauses
in order
to allow
what is read
to sink in
to permeate
one's thoughts

as the purpose
is not to
finish a book
but to have
a writing
one can

come back to
time and again

a place
where
spiritual
nourishment
is always
available

repetition
brings home
what is
expressed
until it
becomes a
wellspring
of inspiration
and refreshment
whenever
needed

selah

Rev. Peter L. Chabot, M.M.

Mary with Child, John the Baptist and Angels
Polidoro de Renzi
1515-1565

I in 1886
a touring
opera company
was to
perform
a most difficult
and demanding
opera
before a
packed house in
Rio de Janeiro

dismaying news
swept through
the crowd
the conductor
had taken ill

there would be
no performance

from a back
orchestra row
an unknown
cellist named
Arturo
put aside
his instrument
and approached
the conductor's
stand

an incredulous
silence
greeted him
he picked
up the baton

tapped
for attention
and directed
Aida
from memory

at the curtain
two hours later
accompanied by
thunderous
applause the
Toscanini
legend
had been born

and a lesson
reinforced
on the value
of preparedness

when the
Master returns

many will not
be prepared
some will be
a few will be
well prepared

in what group
do i
want to be

Mary with Jesus, Mary Magdalen and a Donor
Lucas von Leyden
1494-1533

*I*n the
movie

Lili

Leslie Caron
gives a
winsome
performance
as an
orphaned waif
who joins
a circus

loneliness
and unhappiness
begin to
weigh
her down

her only friends
are the puppets
to whom she
pours out
her soul
and receives
solace and
consolation
in their
friendship
and concern

she decides
to leave
the circus
but first
goes to
say goodbye

to the puppets
they are all
very sad
and try
to persuade
her to stay

in the midst
of this
a realization
takes place
these are
only puppets
she reaches
behind them
and draws
the curtain

revealing
the puppeteer

a young man
with the circus
who is
in love
with her

God is
behind all
creation
He loves each
one of us
in a measure
we can scarcely
imagine and
seeks our love
in return

Rev. Peter L. Chabot, M.M.

Madonna and Child
Hans Memling
1435-1494

A Tree
Grows In
Brooklyn
is a story
of a certain
kind of tree
that thrives
amid
asphalt streets
cement
sidewalks
overgrown
vacant lots
things that
come to
mind when
one thinks
of inner city

but this one
is comfortable
there
seems
right
at home
and flourishes
like
the palm tree
in the psalm
but under
less promising
conditions

faith
can do

the same

in hardship
it sends
its roots
deeper

given
half a chance
and a little care
a crack
in concrete
an opening
in difficult
situations
is all
it needs
to crowd through
and grow
to maturity

Lord
strengthen
our faith
make it
bear fruit
unto
eternal life

Theotokos Panachranta
11th Century Illumination from the Gertrude Psalter

a Special
Olympics race
was going
to take place
in wheelchairs

there was a
lot of publicity

the winner
would get
a scholarship
and most likely
have their
profile etched
on the
medal itself
as the committee
searched for an
inspirational
image to capture
the spirit
of the event

the race started
the favorite
gained an
early lead
was winning
handily
when she noticed
a companion
in trouble

she went
over to help

(it was
important
to each just
to finish
because you
got a ribbon
for that)

however
stopping
to help
cost her
the race

but

the two of them
did finish
last and
next to last

and this was
the scene
the committee
forged on
the medal

and the last
shall be first

Rev. Peter L. Chabot, M.M.

The Visitation
Jaques Daret
1404-1470

a
bamboo-like
plant
common
to the
rain forest
has slow growth
for a year or so

then its
development
is phenomenal

that's because
it first lays out
an extensive
network
of roots
that feed into
the stalk
giving it
stability
nourishment
toughness
endurance

the
spiritual rule
follows
this basic
procedure
and practice
so that
it does not
have to

depend on
mood
emotion
feeling
but can
and must
operate
in dryness
boredom
trial
suffering
in a
routine
that has been
set up and
fortified
to carry one
through
hard times

as a
wise old monk
once said

you keep
the rule
and the rule
will keep
you

Early Morning Meditations

Madonna and Child
Duccio Buoninsegna
1255-1318

a good
way of
praying
during
dryness
distraction
temptation

even during
meditational
reading
if the mind
wanders

is to
take the
rosary beads
and use them
for a series
of shorter
prayers

Jesus Mary
i love thee
save souls

my Lord
my God
and my all

the holy names
Jesus and Mary
said slowly
and reflectively
are prayers
in themselves

they
weather storms
build
inner strength
keep us focused
on our
prime purpose

to know
love
and
serve God
in this life
so as
to be
happy
with Him
for all
eternity

prayer
is the
trail mix
for this
perilous
and arduous
journey

Rev. Peter L. Chabot, M.M.

Benois Madonna
Leonardo da Vinci
1452–1519

a young man
walked into
a telegraph
office to
answer a
help wanted
sign
in the window

he sat there
for a
brief time
then got up
went to a
closed door
knocked
and went in

a few
moments later
he came out
with the manager
who explained
to others waiting
that
the position
had been
filled

those waiting
to apply
were upset
at this
apparent
unfairness
in that the
person hired

did not wait
his turn

listen
the manager said

(in the background
a telegraph
key was
incessantly
clicking
transmitting
a message)

if you can
decode that
go to
the closed door
knock
and enter
you are hired

Lord Jesus
help us
to stay alert
for your
messages
then read
and follow them

Early Morning Meditations

Theotokos of Tolga
13th Century Russian Icon

a famous
violinist
was approached
after a concert
and told

i would
give a lifetime
to play like that

the response was
i have

including
a lifetime
of dedication
and practice

performing
at that level
if even
a day goes by
without
practice
it is noticeable
for the
fire inside
burns just
a tiny bit
lower

if two days
go by
one's colleagues
notice
three days
and the audience

is aware
that something
is amiss

prayer follows
the same
pattern
the danger being
a drift
toward
the backwaters
of very little
or none at all

o Blessed Mother
help us to
prayerfully
keep spiritual
commitments
alive
pondering them
in our hearts
that they
may be
light
life
and strength
for our
journey home

Rev. Peter L. Chabot, M.M.

Madonna and Child
Pompeo Batoni
1708-1787

an old
movie
had a
newly
married
couple
on the deck
of an
oceangoing
liner

hopes
dreams
the thousand
things
that are
talked about
when you are
young
in love
and life
is unfolding
before you

romantic
moonlight
surrounded
that fragile
bubble
of a moment
one thinks
might go on
forever

they lingered
briefly

then moved away
from the rail

i'll never forget
the jarring impact
of the
next scene

a life preserver
hanging there
with a
single word
on it

Titanic

ominously
speeding
to its
tragic
rendezvous
with a
massive
mountain
of ice
waiting there
dead ahead

watch and pray
for you
know not
the day
or the hour

Early Morning Meditations

Madonna Tempi
Raphael Santi (Raphael)
1484-1520

an employee
in a huge
department
store

carrying
a tray
of
price tags

laid out
precisely
and in order

dropped
the tray

the tags
scattered
were
scooped up
and applied
randomly

so that
expensive goods
went for
almost nothing

and trinkets
commanded
enormous
prices

in the
world today
values are
likewise

turned
upside down
inside out

eternal values
lie unappreciated
in low esteem

while
passing fads
rule the day

Lord Jesus
grant us
discernment
to seek
and find
what is
most important

like Mary
seated at
your feet
choosing the
best part
that shall not
be taken
away

Rev. Peter L. Chabot, M.M.

Refuge of Sinners
Luigi Crosio
1835-1915

*L*istings
of names
are everywhere

usually of
those who
have made
significant
contributions
to a town
state
or nation

founders of
organizations
honor rolls
of famous
men and women

names that
go way back
in history
names from
recent times

names long
remembered
names soon
forgotten

some enshrined
on memorials
like that at
Pearl Harbor
and on the
monument

to those
who died there

but the
most important
listing
by far
is the list
of those
of all times
and all ages
who are
inscribed
in the

Book of Life

awaiting
final judgment
on those
who are saved
and on those
who are not

and only
those whose
names
are written
in the
Book of Life
shall enter

Early Morning Meditations

Madonna
Don Lorenzo Monaco
1370-1425

A a best selling
book on travel
had an
unusual title
it advised
where

not to go

political unrest
unsafe water
imprisonment
accidents
sickness
lost or stolen
passports
all sorts
of things
that could
turn vacations
into nightmares

there are
similar
elements
lying hid
in every
human experience

brigands
along the
way of this
earthly journey
who would
rob one
of life itself

so that
half the
journey
is spent just
staying out of
wrong places

the phrase
occasions of sin
covers
the same
ground
in the
spiritual life

the elimination
insofar
as possible
of those
destructive
forces

influences
that can
leave
mere good
intentions
in ruins

Lord help
us to live here
in such a way
as to live
hereafter
in heaven

Rev. Peter L. Chabot, M.M.

Madonna and Child
Jorg Breu the Younger
1510-1547

Lessons
on prayer
are taught
not only
in books
and lives of
the saints

i was
passing by a
street vendor
her wares
were stored
in a wooden
suitcase
propped open
and held at
waist level
by a
makeshift
tripod

she sold
candles
matches
candy
things
you'd have
to sell
a lot of
in order to
make any
kind of profit

so you'd
expect

a sales pitch
on walking by

instead
i found her
entirely
absorbed
in a small
booklet

curious
i glanced
at the title

it was a
collection
of novena
prayers

that
simple but
eloquent
scene
remains
with me
as an
impressive
lesson on

where
when
and how
to pray

Early Morning Meditations

Thronende Madonna
Italo-Byzantinischer Maler
13th Century

a statue of
Christ in the
Andes

is lighted
at night
it can
be seen
far and wide
and from
way out at sea
perched
on its high
mountain peak

it was forged
from melted
down cannons
and placed
on the border
between Chile
and Argentina
as a pledge
that there would
be peace
forevermore
between the
two nations

and so
it has been
and so
it will be
because
this statue
represents

the only One
who can
guarantee
and maintain
enduring peace

it is but a
glimmer
of a time
when swords
will be beaten
into plowshares
and spears
into
pruning hooks

when there
will be peace
on all my
holy mountain

let us
work toward
and pray for
the time
when
these promises
will universally
come true

Rev. Peter L. Chabot, M.M.

Marriage at Cana
Giotto Di Bondone
1266-1337

every
South American
city and
good sized
town has a
plaza
at its center

an acre
or more
of trees
and fountains
park benches
leisurely
walkways
where birds sing
and children play

all this
right
in the midst
of the most
valuable
real estate
around

the people
recognizing
the need
for a place
of repose
rest
tranquility
space

located in
the center

of all the
surrounding
busyness

our lives
need a
quiet center
of calm
of prayer
where we can
commune
with God
be aware
of his presence
recharge
our spiritual
energies

come aside
our Lord
tells us
and
rest
a while

Early Morning Meditations

Birth of the Virgin
Francisco Zurburan
1598-1664

untold dollar
millions are
lying about
just waiting
to be claimed
before they
revert back
to state or
local funds

bank accounts
safety deposits
stock dividends
treasures
buried or
hidden
never found
or dug up

policies
benefits
forgotten
neglected

opportunities
forever lost
that could have
made a
big difference

the same
occurs a
hundredfold
over in the
spiritual
realm

prayers
not said
a good deed
not done
a kind word
not spoken

wasted time
that could have
been spent in
meditation
or attainment of
spiritual riches

in applying for
working toward
laying up
treasure
in heaven

that cannot
be lost
stolen
forgotten
destroyed

but the
good news is
amendment
can be made

all this
can still
happen

Rev. Peter L. Chabot, M.M.

Blessed Virgin with Jesus
Unknown Artist

Ballast
is an
important
element
in sailing
needed
for stability

too little
and a ship
can become
top heavy
liable
to capsize

an ore freighter
once left port
with the cargo
distributed
unevenly
in the hold

a storm arose
rocked the vessel
shifted the bulk
of contents
to one side

and it
went down
with the loss
of all personnel

the spiritual life
likewise
must
be steadied

kept on
an even keel
guided
by sound
principles

it needs
the weight
of much
prayer
and penance

consistent
rather than
sporadic
employment
of these
spiritual arms
in the
contest with
the forces
of evil

but its weight
is the
stronger force
and will
prevail

Early Morning Meditations

Virgin of Guadalupe
18th Century, Mexican School

Lord
are there
few saved

will i be
what will
be my
final destiny

some few
have had
this answered
in their lifetime

the thief
on the cross
to whom
Jesus said
today
you shall be
with Me
in paradise

the apostles
on return
from their
journey
rejoice
in this
that your
names
are written
in heaven

when
a major

purchase
is made
a down
payment
brings
possession

keys to a
new car
the deed
for a house
bestow ownership

as long as
the payments
are kept up

so
we have
salvation
we are saved
we have
this most
priceless of
all treasures
it is ours
to keep

as long as
we keep up
the payments

103

Rev. Peter L. Chabot, M.M.

Assumption of the Blessed Virgin Mary
El Greco
1541-1614

one method
in long usage
for keeping
water from
spilling
out of a
pail
carried
some distance
is to
float a
piece of wood
on the water
surface

this keeps
the water
calm
and prevents
it from
sloshing
around

the wood
of the cross
has the
same effect
on one's life

it stabilizes
pacifies
prevents
spilling
and loss

the cross
of Jesus

has this
effect
a constant
reminder
of the immensity
of God's love
and the price
our Lord
paid for
our ransom

it keeps
our true purpose
in life
constantly
in mind
and provides
the incentive
and strength
to attain it

we adore Thee
o Christ
and we praise
Thee
because by
thy holy cross
Thou hast
redeemed
the world

The Fountain of Life
Hans Holbein the Younger
1498-1543

a young
adventurer
stirred by
tales of
faraway lands
and exotic places
went to sea
time passed
and he absorbed
the routine
of sea life

one day
he was assigned
to the crow's nest
to watch for
passing ships
or signs of land

the sea
was rough
as he climbed
the perch above
seemed a
long way off

he continued
but made
the mistake
of looking down
the ropes
were swaying
he was losing
his grip
as the ship
swayed
back and forth

an old sea hand
realizing
from down below
what was
happening
yelled
look up lad!

he did
and was able
to continue
the climb
till he reached
safety

in life's journey
we are also
bidden to
look up
keep our
gaze above
whence help
will come
from on high

may the
Lord of our
life and journey
guide us
through
the storms
and rough seas
of life
and safely
into home port

Rev. Peter L. Chabot, M.M.

Madonna and Child Enthroned
Margaritone d'Arezzo
1216-1290

stories
and legends
that endure
do so
because there
is an element
of truth
to them
something
that speaks
to the human
and says
this is true
learn from it

Damocles
was invited
to a banquet
he was given
a place
of honor

the festivities
began
with pomp
and spectacle
of a royal feast

an uneasiness
came over him

looking up
he saw
a heavy
sharp sword
over his head

suspended
by a
single thread

all earthly
treasures
and pleasures
depended
on how long
that thread
would
hold

good
human wisdom
is also
good
spiritual wisdom

watch
and pray
for you know not
when the
Son of Man
will come

be on guard
be vigilant
lest
He find
you asleep
when He does

Early Morning Meditations

Black Madonna Fresco
Axum Cathedral, Ethiopia

a war galley
stopped
in Algeria
giving
brief respite
to a hundred
beaten and
exhausted
rowers
permanently
chained
to their
floating coffin
amid conditions of
indescribable
squalor

a mercedarian
monk
came aboard
carrying a bag
of jewelry

he bargained for
the release of
as many rowers
as possible

three
the overseer said
he watched hope
rise and die
in a fourth who
if the ship
wasn't sunk
would eventually
broken in health
and in spirit

be cast
overboard

a whispered plea
startled the guard

he unchained
the fourth man
who rose
and left
as if
in a dream

the four waited
to thank
their benefactor
but the monk
did not appear

as the ship
glided past
the fourth man
stared in
through the port-
hole
saw someone
shackled in his
former place

it was the monk
he was in leg irons
he was rowing

the galley
pulled away
and headed
into battle

Rev. Peter L. Chabot, M.M.

Madonna and Child
Anton Raphael Mengs
1728-1779

for a
certain
kind of
banana
plant
a lot of
rain is
needed

then
a dry
spell

so the
tap root
will
go deep
seeking
nourishment
and stability

otherwise
it will
stay near
the surface
with little
nutriment
and depth
to hold it
steady

the
spiritual
life is
like this
in that
early
consolations

draw one
into the
realm
of the spirit
but the roots
must
go deeper
for stability
and
sustenance
for the
time when
surface
emotions
will have
dried up
and can
no longer
be depended
upon

Lord
may your
Word
sink
deep roots
in my life
and bear
much fruit
in time
and eternity

Mother of God
Svitozar Nenyuk
1962-

the second
battle of
the Marne
figures
prominently
in military
history

it was the
final and
decisive conflict
of World War I
where
aided by
the presence of
American troops
Marshal Foch
repulsed an
enemy attack
took the
offensive
and brought
an end
to the fighting

an eye witness
had as a
most vivid
remembrance of
the field marshal

a glimpse
of him kneeling
before the
tabernacle
in a village church
before going
into battle

our spiritual
journey
is also
a warfare
often
described
as spiritual
combat

and
its most
powerful weapon
is likewise
kneeling
before the
tabernacle
in a village
church
before going
into battle

Rev. Peter L. Chabot, M.M.

Madonna and Child with St. John The Baptist, Two Saints and Donors
Vincenzo di Biagio Catena
1480-1531

a will
is being read
you can hear
a pin drop

the inheritance
is being
divided

gasps
groans
sounds of
delight mixed
with muttered
anger

on and on
it goes
a lot
of people
are there

each given
something
or nothing

elation on the
part of some
receiving
a reward
for their
friendship and
loyalty

for others
only anguish
and remorse
as they realize

it is now
too late
to make amends

our inheritance
will be read out
one day
in the presence
of all

now
is the time
to do something
about it

if we wait
till then
it will be
too late

Lord
help us
to make this
the most important
task of
our lives

for our everything
depends
upon it

Mary
Agnollo Bronzino
1503-1572

Joe Louis
was asked
about an
up-and-coming
young fighter

he replied:
he can hit
he can take a
punch
he keeps
in training

what more
do you want

that pretty well
covers it

there is a
similar pattern
in the
spiritual life

prayer
penance
perseverance

fit one for
the spiritual fight
by a
day-to-day
implementation
of these
principles

a strong
prayer life

moves one
into the spiritual
dimension
draws upon
a power beyond
human resources
for these alone
are sadly
deficient

it needs to be
ingrained
habitual
become a
way of life
a constant
mode of conduct

Lord
help us
to stay in
spiritual shape
to keep
in training
to fight
the good fight
and obtain
the reward
of eternal life

Rev. Peter L. Chabot, M.M.

Pieta
Vincent van Gogh
1853-1890

restoring
a masterpiece
of painting
is a
painstaking job

it must be cleansed
of dirt and grime

sometimes an
amateurish overlay
must be removed
without damaging
the original

colors must be
brought back
to pristine
condition

then it is housed
in an elegant
renaissance frame
given ample space
with overhead light
on a museum wall

a descriptive
plaque
is placed
alongside
in a
setting appropriate
to its renewed
beauty and
grandeur

the sacrament
of reconciliation
is like this

the recovery
and restoration
of the original
grace and beauty
of a soul
marred by
ravages of sin
made good
as new
time and
time again
even when lost
and seemingly
beyond repair

Lord Jesus
help us to
appreciate more
this sacrament
of your pardon
and peace

and to receive it
more often

Adoration of the Magi
Peter Fransz de Grebber
1600-1652

mist
rising from
the river
near a
small airport
on the
border
between
Bolivia
and Brazil
obscures the
landscape
until
early morning

then it lifts
for about
an hour
allowing
takeoffs and
landings
(first making sure
no cows
are grazing
on it)
before it
sometimes
closes in
again

there are
favorable
moments
for prayer
also

when the mist
of fatigue
worry and
preoccupation
leave the soul
relatively free
from hindrance

prayer is often
crowded into
busy schedules

said on the run
between
activities

this is good
but prime time
is also needed

for if time
is made
for prayer
all the rest
falls into place

Mother Mary
teach us
to pray
keep us in
a prayerful
attitude

Rev. Peter L. Chabot, M.M.

The Annunciation
Antonello da Messina
1430-1479

J. Paul Getty
once the
wealthiest man
on the planet
had a
three-point
sure-fire
formula
for getting rich

go to bed early
get up early
strike oil

this last
of course
is subject to
the vagaries
of accident
and circumstance
surrounding all
strike-it-rich
plans
and projects

the attainment
of the most
valuable goal
and treasure
of all

life with God
here and
hereafter

is no accident
but follows
a program to

seek first
the kingdom
of God

do all that
is required
to gain it

avoid whatever
stands
in the way

Lord Jesus
our guide
and our goal
keep us focused
on the
one thing necessary

grant us
the grace
needed
in our pursuit
of it

lead us
past the obstacles
to a happy
possession

The Annunciation
Auguste Pichon
1805–1900

a highlander
bagpipe player
was asked
to give some
renditions

which he did
the call to colors
some marching
tunes and
a few others

then someone
asked him
to play a retreat

nah
he said
i never learned
a retreat

what an
attitude

no provision
made for
things falling
apart

total concentration
geared toward
success in battle

this is the
attitude of faith
that sees
only victory
in sight

and confidence
in the means
to attain it

based on
Jesus' promise
in the world
you will
have affliction
but take courage
I have
overcome
the world

being united
to Jesus Christ
is our
assurance
of victory

only in
His saving power
is our guarantee
of future
beatitude

Lord
help us
keep our
gaze on You
and the prize
of eternal life
we can begin
to enjoy
in this one

Rev. Peter L. Chabot, M.M.

Assumption of the Virgin
Pierre Paul Prud'hon
1758-1823

*Y*ears ago
a prominent
businessman
was walking
down a street
in Stockholm

he bought
a newspaper
and was
jolted by the
(mistaken)
appearance
of his own
obituary

he kept
reading
to find out
what people
thought of him
his financial
success
the power
attendant
upon it

here was
a man
the article
droned on
who devoted
his life
to making
weapons of war

this stopped him
in his tracks

from then on
his time
energy
and fortune
were used
exclusively
for the betterment
of humanity

providing
prizes and
incentives
for advancement
in the arts
and sciences

the most prestigious
award going
for the cause
of peace

so it was
that
Alfred Nobel
formerly associated
with war
now became known
as an
advocate for peace

how will
my obituary
read

do i
want to
change it

The Deposition
Nicholas Poussin
1594–1665

a thief
left his
car running
ran into
a convenience
store
waved a pistol
stuffed bills
into his
pocket
robbed customers
scooped
cans of food
into a bag
and backed
out the door

he turned
and stopped
incredulous

someone
had stolen
his car

so there
he was
a ridiculous
figure
wearing
a ski mask
in the middle
of summer
arms full
of stolen goods
in a neighborhood
suddenly

turned hostile

the faint sound
of a siren
is heard
in the distance

he drops everything
and starts
running
the homes
all seem
to have gates
and high fences
and barking dogs

eyes peer
out of windows
he'd be lucky
to be able to hide
somewhere
and escape
under cover
of darkness

'all things
betrayest thee
who betrayest
Me'

Rev. Peter L. Chabot, M.M.

The Holy Family
Raphael
1483-1520

an ancient
fable
has a lion
inviting
a fox
to dinner
in his den

the fox
demurs
no thank
you sir
for i see
a great many
tracks
leading
into your den
but none
coming out

stray animals
passing
along
the Nile
drink the
water
hurriedly
on the run
because
crocodiles
hiding in
the shoreline
weeds
can strike
surprisingly
fast

modern
technology
has done
much good
but it has
also brought
the lion's den
and
dangerous waters
into our
homes
just a
click away

dear Lord
help us
in our
constant effort
to do Your will
to keep Your law
aid us
with Your grace
help us rise
if we fall

in Jesus' name
amen

Virgin and Child with Two Angels
Andrea del Verrocchio
1435-1488

at the edge
of the
Sahara desert
in Morocco
is a lonely
outpost
of the
French Foreign
Legion

the stone archway
over the
main gate
has three
Latin words

Legio
Patria Est

the Legion
is our Fatherland

home
to exiles
wanderers
those looking
for someone or
something
to render
commitment to
an allegiance
that would
dominate
demand
every moment
of their lives
perhaps even
their deaths

but in
return
would grant
them
an identity
a sense
of belonging
a cause
in which
they would
find
purpose and
meaning
for lives
that hitherto
had been
aimless or
poured out
in dissipation

the Church
fills this role
on the spiritual
plain
demanding all
giving all
and more
in return

the Church
is our Mother

Rev. Peter L. Chabot, M.M.

The Virgin with Angels
Adolphe Bouguereau
1825-1905

amartia
is a Greek word
for sin
it means
to miss
the mark
to fail
to accomplish
one's purpose
in life

by deliberately
doing
something
that renders
accomplishing
it impossible

school yearbooks
usually have
'most likely
to succeed'
under
someone's picture
hopes and dreams
waiting to be
fulfilled

many a
success story
carries with it
the satisfaction
of having
accomplished
this goal
many stories
do not

there is
one quest though
one aim
that soars above
all others

to attain
salvation
to come
to a knowledge
of Jesus Christ
and live
the new life
He gives

reach this
and all
is won

miss this mark
lose out here
and words
cannot begin
to describe
the enormity
of the loss

The Visitation
Jacopo Pontormo
1494–1556

a child
is standing
alone
scared
trembling
on a dock

her family is on
the leaving boat

she hears
her father's voice
when we pass
where you are
jump
and I will
catch you

but daddy
it's dark
and I can't
see you

that doesn't
matter
i can see you

so jump!

which she does

an awkward
desperate
ungainly
scared-little-kid
kind of jump
but to her father

the most beautiful
sight in the world

it takes her
across deadly
murky waters
waiting below
it takes everything
she has
holding nothing back
and is just enough

it lands her
safely in her
father's arms
sobbing
and trembling
her frightened
tears
mingling with
the relieved ones
streaming
down his face
as they cling
to each other

belief in God
needs a leap
of faith
leaving all
to gain all
as it lands us
in the
waiting arms
of God

Rev. Peter L. Chabot, M.M.

Virgin and Child and Angel Musicians
Piero di Cosimo
1462-1521

the new
base commander
arriving at
his post
saw a
gallows
prominently
displayed
in the
assembly area

there would
be a
hanging
the next
morning

it had been
ordered
by the
previous
administration
so there
was nothing
he could
do about it

his authority
did not extend
to countermanding
existing orders

but he
did not
want to start
his tenure
with a hanging

he was
however
in charge
of the fort
and all its
provisions

and he
did have a fireplace
in his quarters

and it did
get cold
during
the winter

so he
requisitioned
the wood
of the gallows
and ordered
that it be
sawed
into one foot
lengths
for his fireplace

is there
anything
in my life
that should be
turned into
firewood

Virgin of the Silver Spring
Svitozar Nenyuk
1962-

the rain forest
is a world of
endless rivers
winding through
vast stretches
of tropical jungle

four Maryknoll
boats working
this area
each carry
a title of
Our Blessed Mother
a kind of
floating litany
invoking
her protection

visits to those
living in
these environs
would include
Mass by lantern
and candlelight
baptisms
marriages
blessings for
as long as
necessary
all the needed
accessories
having been
conveyed from
the boat by a
noisily chattering
group of youngsters
lantern light
illuminating their

happy faces

a bicycle generator
was used
to show slides

the last
slide shown
was of our
Risen Lord
standing on
the shore of Galilee
calling to
his apostles who
are coming in
by boat

we are all
in that scene
the Lord stands
on the shore
of our lives
calling
inviting each
to live
a new life
in his name
and to share this
with others

Lord Jesus
help us hear
and respond
to your call

Mother Mary
help us
live it

Rev. Peter L. Chabot, M.M.

Madonna and Child
Sandro Botticelli
1445-1510

An often
overlooked fact
regarding prayer
is that it
carries within
the answer
to what it seeks
and always obtains
more than
is asked for

being able
to turn to God
in faith hope
and love is an
incomparable gift
and privilege
in itself
being not only
a gracious concession
but a royal
invitation
even a command

come to me
Our Lord tells us
ask seek knock

prayer is a
haven of peace
and tranquility
it lifts one up
in weakness
gives rest
in fatigue
is a healing
ointment
for pain
brings comfort

in grief
light in darkness

it heals wounds
mends broken
hearts
is an oasis
in desert places
a stronghold
in danger
a safe harbor mid
storm-tossed seas
a garden of calm
in midst of strife

all it needs
is an opening
of the door
of one's heart
to the gentle
steady
insistent
knocking
of the Lord

Lord Jesus
come into
my home
as its most
honored guest
make of it
a house of prayer
and please grant
that i may be
welcome in yours
through all eternity

i thank You

Adoration in the Forest
Filippo Lippi
1480-1556

during
one of
his visits
to the US
John Paul II
stopped by
a seminary
to make a
visit to the
Blessed Sacrament

security
entered the
chapel first
with two
German shepherds

(their main job
being to detect
any hidden
presence)

they
energetically
inspected here
and there
quickly
and efficiently

as they approached
the tabernacle
where the
Blessed Sacrament
was reserved
their movements
became slower
and slower

and then
they froze

their handlers
had to come in
and lead them
away
no one else
could move them

an extraordinary
witness
and homage
to the presence
of the Lord
where so many
heedlessly
pass by

Lord Jesus
make us
more conscious
of your presence

in your Sacrament
in your Word
in the world
in others
in ourselves

Rev. Peter L. Chabot, M.M.

Altarpiece of the Halbernd
Lorenzo Lotto
1480-1556

on a
spiritual
renewal program
in the
Holy Land
a concelebrated
Mass was
held at
the site of
the Last Supper
in the Cenacle
in Jerusalem

the homilist
in a few words
described
the scene
in phrases
that still
linger
in my
memory

here
he said

here
is where
it all
happened

here
Jesus gave
his farewell
discourse
instituted
the Eucharist

left for
Gethsemane
to begin his
sorrowful
Passion

here
he appears
to his disciples
after the
Resurrection

here
Pentecost
the coming
of the
Holy Spirit
took place

Lord
grant us a
renewed
appreciation
of Holy Mass

help us
see it
as the Last Supper
your Passion
Death
Resurrection
and Presence
here
in our own time
in our own lives

Assumption of the Virgin
Titian
1488-1576

"there is
no problem
however great
that cannot
be resolved
by the recitation
of the Rosary"

thus spoke
Sister Lucy
one of those
favored few
who have
conversed with
Our Lady
while still
in this earthly
existence

imagine
what would
happen
if a promise
like this
were offered
to the worldly

do this
and all
your cares
and deepest needs
will be
taken care of

no sacrifice
would be
too great

to obtain it
yet most
let this
and similar
promises

'whoever dies
clothed in this
scapular
shall not suffer
eternal fire'

pass them by

letting the
most important things
slip away
in a chase
after trifles

Blessed Mother
open our eyes
to the wonder
of your promises
open our hearts
to your
great love for us
that we
may respond
in kind
and live
as your children
on earth
as we hope to
live forever
in heaven

Rev. Peter L. Chabot, M.M.

Assumption of the Virgin Mary
Peter Paul Rubens
1577-1640

the small
adobe chapel
was full
the mood
was reverent
quiet

flickering
candles
and a
lantern
provided
the only
light
as i
vested
for Mass

smoke from
smoldering
damp straw
in a half-gourd
in the doorway
kept away
some of
the mosquitoes

nursing mothers
swished
cloths
back and forth
over the heads
of their infants
to protect them

distractions
in prayer

are like
mosquitoes
there's
not much
you can do
about them
other than
try to reduce
their number

if they
persist
are troubling
or of import

make
a prayer
out of them

ask for
deliverance
an answer
the ability
to cope
to see
this through

Lord Jesus
Mother Mary
grant me
prayer that
comes from
attention
of the mind
and depth
of the heart

Early Morning Meditations

Barbadori Altarpiece
Filippo Lippi
1406–1469

a plaintive tune
'yesterday
when I was
young'
sings a sad
remembrance
of dissolution
and endless
partying
heedless of
the days
of youth
ebbing away
encroaching age
comes in
somber colors
mourning
opportunities
that have fled
down the
corridors of
a misspent life
with only
bittersweet
memories
remaining
of those
wasted yesterdays
when i
was young

but all
is not lost
in the parable
of the workers
in the marketplace

the householder
goes out at
the eleventh hour
to hire laborers

for with God
there is still
one last chance

even as
the sands of life
are running out
i can still
arise
and go home
to the Father

one last chance
to clamber
aboard
even as the train
is leaving
the station

if i act
now

Rev. Peter L. Chabot, M.M.

Canigiani Holy Family
Raphael
1483-1520

to really
appreciate
the Statue
of Liberty
you have to
behold her
through the
tear filled eyes
of immigrants
coming in
on one-way
tickets
all their
belongings
contained
in a few
cardboard
suitcases

looking up
at this
kindly angel
welcoming them
to the land
of their dreams

you have to
see her
from the
point of view
of veterans
returning from
foreign wars

while many
a comrade
lie buried

far from home

entrance
into the
kingdom
of God
is like this
but on the
highest possible
level

a journey
to freedom
from an
old way of life
freedom
from bondage
to sin

pledging allegiance
to a new homeland
accepting
concomitant
duties
privileges
responsibilities

Father
grant us entrance
into your kingdom
and the grace
to remain there

in Jesus' name
amen

Early Morning Meditations

Castelfranco Madonna
Giorgione
1477-1510

life and art
intermingle
in the works of
Mary Cassatt
an American
artist whose
contributions to
Impressionism
were rich and full
and deeply felt
even to
the present day

her study of
the Masters
shows its influence
but in a style
uniquely
her own

women and
children in
daily life
provide
many a theme
in her portrayals
as she captures
the mystery
and grandeur
in ordinary things
everyday happenings

not all are
called to be
great artists
but all
are called

to holiness

and as art
enhances the
ordinary
holiness
enhances the
human

progress in
the spiritual life
is a blend
of God's grace
one's own efforts
and the influence
of teachers
and guides

each saint
retains the qualities
with which they
have been blessed
but now suffused
with the luminosity
of holiness

Mother Mary
help and guide us
your children
to all we are
meant to be
help us to
shine forth
the holiness
of God
in our lives

Rev. Peter L. Chabot, M.M.

Contarini Madonna
Giovanni Bellini
1430-1516

The Cure of Ars
kept noticing
an old
peasant
just sitting
or kneeling
before the
tabernacle
or crucifix

doing
this often
and for
long periods
of time
evidence
of a
high degree
of prayer

so what
do you say
to Our Lord
he asked him
one day

you don't
seem to
be using
any book
of prayers

no
the old fellow
said
i just
look at Him

and He
looks at me

a classic
definition
of prayer is
raising
the mind
and heart
to God
in faith
hope
and love

the more deeply
one enters
into the
ways of prayer
the simpler
it becomes
until
what is left
is a simple
gaze
of love
for
God is love

Holy Spirit
help us
to pray
as we ought
help us
to pray more